Funnier Bone Jokes

Corny Thanksgiving JOKES to Tickle Your FUNNY BONE

Linda Bozzo

Enslow Elementary
an imprint of
Enslow Publishers, Inc.
40 Industrial Road
Box 398
Berkeley Heights, NJ 07922
USA
http://www.enslow.com

Enslow Elementary, an imprint of Enslow Publishers, Inc.

Enslow Elementary® is a registered trademark of Enslow Publishers, Inc.

Library of Congress Cataloging-in-Publication Data

Bozzo, Linda.

Corny Thanksgiving jokes to tickle your funny bone / Linda Bozzo.

p. cm. — (Fünnier bone jokes)

Includes index.

Summary: "Read jokes, limericks, tongue twisters, and knock-knock jokes about Thanksgiving. Also find out fun facts about the holiday"—Provided by publisher.

ISBN 978-0-7660-4120-2

1. Thanksgiving Day—Juvenile humor. I. Title.

PN6231.T566B69 2013

818'.602—dc23

2012007702

Future editions:

Paperback ISBN 978-1-4644-0178-7

ePUB ISBN 978-1-4645-1091-5

PDF ISBN 978-1-4646-1091-2

Printed in the United States of America

082012 Lake Book Manufacturing, Inc., Melrose Park, IL

10 9 8 7 6 5 4 3 2 1

To Our Readers: We have done our best to make sure all Internet Addresses in this book were active and appropriate when we went to press. However, the author and the publisher have no control over and assume no liability for the material available on those Internet sites or on other Web sites they may link to. Any comments or suggestions can be sent by e-mail to comments@enslow.com or to the address on the back cover.

Every effort has been made to locate all copyright holders of material used in this book. If any errors or omissions have occurred, corrections will be made in future editions of this book.

Enslow Publishers, Inc., is committed to printing our books on recycled paper. The paper in every book contains 10% to 30% post-consumer waste (PCW). The cover board on the outside of each book contains 100% PCW. Our goal is to do our part to help young people and the environment too!

Illustration Credits: Clipart.com, pp. 4 (top), 5 (top), 6 (bottom), 7 (top), 9, 11 (top), 12 (bottom), 13 (top), 14 (top), 17 (bottom), 19 (top), 20, 23 (bottom), 25 (bottom), 26 (top), 27 (top), 33 (bottom), 34 (bottom), 35 (top), 36, 37 (top), 38 (bottom), 39 (bottom), 40 (top), 41, 43 (bottom), 44 (bottom); Photos.com: Christos Georghiou, p. 39 (top), Dynamic Graphics, pp. 4 (bottom), 14 (bottom), 17 (top), 30 (bottom), greg walter, p. 18 (top), James Horvath, p. 38 (top), Jennet Chua, p. 40 (bottom), Jupiterimages, p. 13 (bottom), Kelly Hironaka, p. 28 (top), Lada Kholosho, p. 44 (top), Maksim Pasko, p. 32 (bottom), moneca, p. 25 (top) Rebecca Lowe, p. 15 (top); Shutterstock.com, pp. 1, 5 (bottom), 6 (top), 7 (bottom), 8, 10, 11 (bottom), 12 (top), 15 (bottom), 16, 18 (bottom), 19 (middle, bottom), 21, 22, 23 (top). 24, 26 (bottom), 27 (bottom), 28 (bottom), 29, 30 (top), 31, 32 (top), 33 (top), 34 (top, middle), 35 (bottom), 37 (bottom), 42, 43 (bottom).

Cover Illustration:

Contents

1 The *Mayflower*

Where did the Pilgrims play cards on the *Mayflower*?

On the deck.

Knock, knock.

Who's there?

Dewey.

Dewey who?

Dewey need a larger ship?

What did the water say to the ship?

Nothing. It just waved.

How did Pilgrims know what time it was?

Plymouth clock.

DID YOU KNOW?

The *Mayflower* set sail from Plymouth, England, in early September 1620, and didn't land until November. With 102 passengers and about 30 crew members on board, the small wooden ship was crowded. The travelers planned to land at the mouth of the Hudson River, where New York City is today. Instead, they landed on the coast of what is now Massachusetts. That's about 200 miles away! They named their new settlement Plymouth, after the name of the town from which they sailed.

Limerick

A young man set sail with his mother
Along with his much younger brother.
Across the big sea
The three would all be—
And crazy they'd drive one another.

How did the *Mayflower* show that it liked Plymouth Rock?

It hugged the shore.

What did the Pilgrims use to bake cakes?

May-flour.

FUN FACT

Did you know that a baby was born on the *Mayflower*? His parents named him Oceanus Hopkins.

Shelly sailed seven ships.

Knock, knock.

Who's there?

Sid.

Sid who?

Sid down, the ship is rocking.

If you drop a white hat over the side of the *Mayflower*, what does it become?

Wet.

Six slick ships should sail soon.

Limerick

There once was a wooden ship,
That sailed on a very long trip.
For sixty-six days
Rough seas with big waves
Made the *Mayflower* ship seasick.

If April showers bring May flowers, what do May flowers bring?

Pilgrims.

Knock, knock.

Who's there?

Landon.

Landon who?

Landon sight!

The Pilgrims' cows came to America on what ship?

The *Moooflower.*

2 Pilgrims

If the Pilgrims were still alive today, what would they be most famous for?

Their age.

Knock knock.

Who's there?

Steven.

Steven who?

Steven the pilgrims are hungry!

Limerick

There was a Pilgrim from Wise
Who couldn't believe his eyes.
The turkey stood up
And drank from his cup.
What a Thanksgiving surprise!

Shy settlers shall sing silly songs on shore.

If two Pilgrims is company, and three is a crowd, what's four and five?

Nine.

FUN FACT

The Pilgrims were looking for a better life in a new land. But did you know they never called themselves Pilgrims? It's true! Believe it or not, these early settlers from England did not have silver buckles on their shoes. They did not wear black clothing, either. The women and girls usually wore skirts, jackets, and aprons. Their favorite colors were thought to be red, blue, purple, and green. The men and older boys wore pants that went to their knees, long shirts, and vests. Until they were six years old, boys wore dresses. Neither women nor men ever wore buckles on their hats, belts, or shoes. Buckles were not used until much later.

Pilgrims picked plenty of perfect plump pumpkins.

Knock, knock.

Who's there?

Evan Chu.

Evan Chu who?

Evan Chu Lee we Pilgrims will land!

Why did the Pilgrim eat a candle?

He only wanted a light snack.

Limerick

There was a Pilgrim from Sledding
Who had to go to a wedding.
He walked to the east,
Three miles at least,
Not knowing where he was heading.

Where did the Pilgrims come from?

Their parents, of course!

What type of music did the Pilgrims like?

Plymouth Rock.

3 The First Thanksgiving

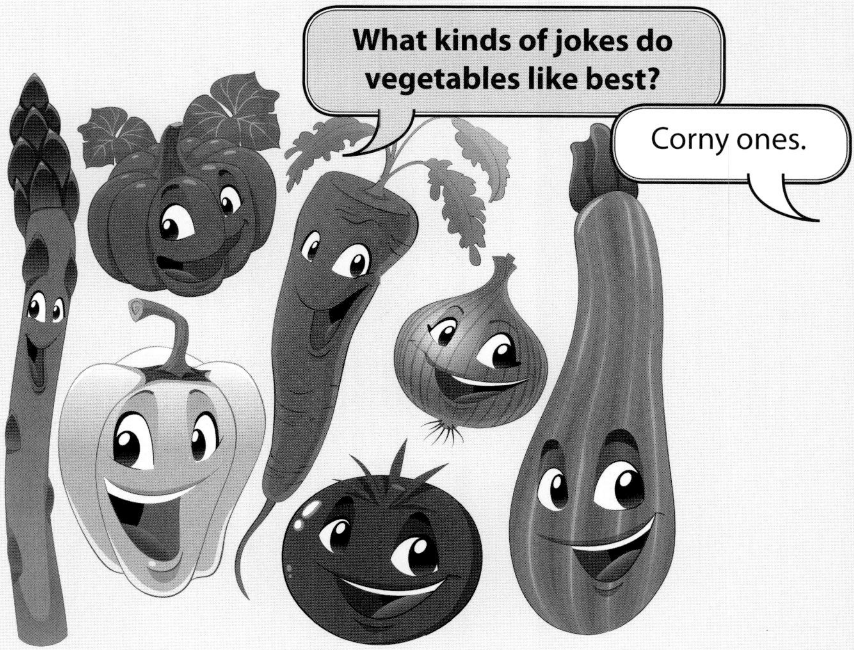

DID YOU KNOW?

During the fall of 1621, the Pilgrims celebrated their harvest feast with Native Americans. The feast lasted three days. They ate, played games, sang, and danced. Did you know it is this harvest feast that is known as the first Thanksgiving? The Pilgrims and Wampanoag Indians had no idea that this celebration would become the oldest holiday in the United States.

What has ears but cannot hear?

A cornfield.

Five fresh fish feasts fed five famished families.

Knock, knock.

Who's there?

Lettuce.

Lettuce who?

Lettuce be thankful for our food.

Why did the cranberries turn so red?

They saw the salad dressing!

Limerick

There was a shy Pilgrim named Jack
Who went to the feast for a snack.
The food he ate
Tasted so great,
He thought he had better go back.

FUN FACT

Today, turkey is what most Americans serve for Thanksgiving dinner. But do you know what types of food were served during the harvest celebration in 1621? We know they ate deer, meat, and fish. We also know they ate wild birds, which may have included turkey. We know they grew corn, squash, and pumpkins. Cranberries grew wild. But there were no sweet potatoes harvested in Plymouth. What about mashed potatoes and cranberry sauce? It might surprise you that these dishes were not even invented yet!

Why didn't the boy get a second helping of turkey?

Because he ate it all the first time.

Where did the first corn come from?

The stalk.

How can you turn a tomato into squash?

Throw it up in the air and let it drop.

Limerick

There once was a Pilgrim named Link
Who caused a super big stink.
From when he was born
He wouldn't eat corn—
Oh, what's a mother to think!

Knock, knock.

Who's there?

Wanda.

Wanda who?

Wanda piece of squash?

Why should you never talk like a turkey?

Because it's rude to use fowl language.

Knock, knock.

Who's there?

Ears.

Ears who?

Ears some more corn.

Four fine fowls flew fast.

4 Thanksgiving Today

What's inside a genie's turkey?

Three wishbones.

Knock, knock.

Who's there?

Henrietta.

Henrietta who?

Henrietta turkey.

What smells the best at Thanksgiving dinner?

Your nose.

Mr. Mush mixes mashed potatoes most Mondays.

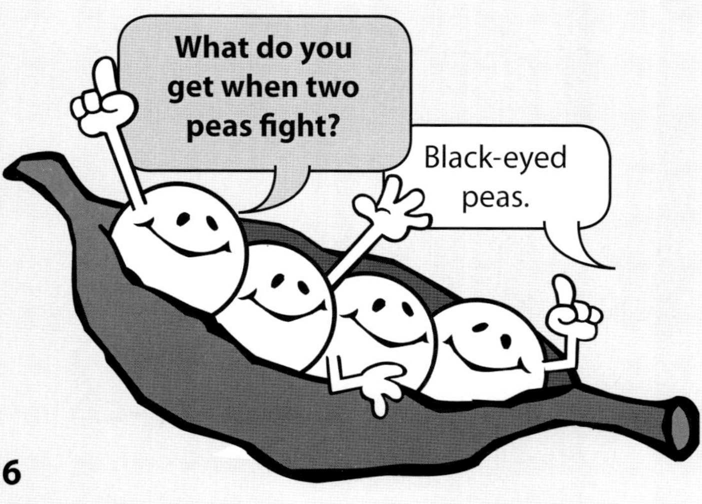

DID YOU KNOW?

Thanksgiving traditions are based on the original 1621 harvest celebration. While the holiday is still a time for giving thanks, the dinner has changed since the early settlers' celebration. Today, favorites include turkey, stuffing, mashed potatoes, vegetables, macaroni and cheese, gravy, cranberry sauce, and pumpkin pie. What does your family eat for Thanksgiving dinner? Since Thanksgiving is a holiday that people of all different backgrounds celebrate, the menu varies from home to home, but the meaning is still the same.

Granny Mary ate cranberries.

What's the difference between the sun and bread?

The sun rises from the east and the bread rises from the yeast.

Limerick

A hungry young lady once said,
"I can never eat enough bread."
We fed her a slice,
Then two slices twice,
Then she asked for some pie instead.

FUN FACT

Did you know that Thanksgiving was not always a national holiday? It's true! In 1863, Abraham Lincoln declared two Thanksgivings. One was held in August. The second, held in November, was to give thanks for the nation's blessings. This fall celebration caught on and has been a tradition ever since. But it wasn't until 1941 that Thanksgiving became a national holiday in the United States. That's when President Franklin D. Roosevelt officially made the fourth Thursday in November Thanksgiving Day.

Limerick

Kevin the cook declared, "Isn't it swell?
My Thanksgiving feast went over quite well.
My mom left early
With dear Aunt Shirley,
Both of them happily stuffed, I could tell."

What's your favorite Thanksgiving vegetable?

Beets me!

Sharon slurps stuffing through special straws.

Knock, knock.
Who's there?
Waddle.
Waddle who?
Waddle I bring for dessert?

What did the baby corn say to the mother corn?
Where's Pop Corn?

Knock, knock.
Who's there?
Owl.
Owl who?
Owl make the stuffing.

5 Pumpkin Pie

Why did the pumpkins have to leave the factory?

They all got canned.

What do you get after eating too much Thanksgiving dinner?

Dessert.

Patty placed pieces of Paul's pumpkin pie on pretty paper plates.

DID YOU KNOW?

Early American settlers might have made a type of pumpkin pie for that first Thanksgiving. It is thought they cut off the top of the pumpkin and cleaned out the insides. Then they filled it with milk, spices, and honey. Did you know that Pilgrims did not have ovens to bake pies in 1621? They cooked the filled pumpkins in hot coals. Pumpkin pie wasn't invented until about fifty years later.

What do you call a guy who gets a pumpkin pie in the face?

Desserted.

Limerick

There was a young lady whose eyes
Grew bigger and bigger in size.
It wasn't until
They got bigger still
That they looked like two pumpkin pies.

Waiter, will the pumpkin pie be long?

No, sir. It will be round.

Knock, knock.

Who's there?

Needle.

Needle who?

Needle piece of pumpkin pie.

Knock, knock.

Who's there?

Leaf.

Leaf who?

Leaf me a piece of pie!

Knock, knock.

Who's there?

Ala.

Ala who?

Pumpkin pie à la mode!

What do you call a fat dessert?

Plumpkin pie.

Peggy picked plenty of perfect pumpkins.

FUN FACT

Did you know, the first canned pumpkin was sold by Libby's in 1929? The recipe that appeared on the label is the same recipe that appears there today. It is probably one of the most popular recipes used to make pumpkin pie at Thanksgiving. Many families serve the pie with whipped cream or à la mode—which means with ice cream on top.

Why was the waiter laughing?

Because the pumpkin pie tasted funny.

What's orange and falls off walls?

Humpty Pumpkin.

Limerick

When Mom tried to bake a pumpkin pie,
The filling got hard and the crust was dry.
The guests threw it out
With a shout and a pout.
Cried Mom, "What a terrible cook am I!"

6 Turkey

Knock, knock.

Who's there?

Tom.

Tom who?

Tom Turkey, that's who.

Why do turkeys always go gobble, gobble?

Because they never learned good table manners.

DID YOU KNOW?

Many people serve turkey for dinner at Thanksgiving and Christmas. But did you know that each year the President of the United States pardons a Thanksgiving turkey? It's true. President George H. W. Bush pardoned the first Thanksgiving turkey on November 14, 1989. Each year since then, the president receives a gift of a live turkey. Instead of having it served for dinner, the president pardons it, or allows it to live. The turkey spends the rest of its natural life living on a farm.

How do turkeys go through the post office?

Bird-class mail.

Gobblers gulp gobs of goopy gravy.

Knock, knock.

Who's there?

Gran.

Gran who?

Granberry dressing for your turkey!

What instrument can turkeys play?

The drums, because they have drumsticks.

How do you eat your turkey dinner?

You gobble it down.

FUN FACTS

Did you know . . .

- Benjamin Franklin wanted to make the wild turkey, not the bald eagle, the national bird of the United States?
- male turkeys are called toms?
- female turkeys are called hens?
- that only male turkeys gobble?
- that female turkeys make a clicking noise?

Limerick

There was a tom turkey who thought
He was much too smart to be caught.
He wore a disguise
That covered his eyes
From a Halloween costume he bought.

Why did the police officers arrest the turkey?

They suspected fowl play.

Knock, knock.

Who's there?

Aida.

Aida who?

Aida lot of turkey.

What do hippies put on their turkey?

Groovy.

What did the turkey say before it was roasted?

I'm stuffed!

Thirty-three thick Thanksgiving turkeys thanked Thelma's quick thinking.

Which side of the turkey has the most feathers?

The outside.

What kind of key can't unlock doors?

Tur-key.

Limerick

There was a plump turkey named Lou.
Each time he ate popcorn he grew.
Whenever he gobbled,
His bird body wobbled.
Oh, what's a wobbling gobbler to do!

7 Thanksgiving Symbols

What's the sleepiest thing at Thanksgiving dinner?

Your nap-kin.

Which weighs more, a pound of fruit or a pound of nuts?

Neither, they both weigh a pound.

Fran fixed fresh flowers and fancy fruit for four favorite friends.

What do police officers eat on Thanksgiving?

Corn on the cop.

Limerick

There was a fair lady named Mabel.
A cornucopia graced her table.
She ate the whole thing
Then started to sing—
For the meal she was certainly grateful.

On which fall holiday do you play a lot of jokes on people?

Pranks-giving.

DID YOU KNOW?

Thanksgiving has many symbols, including turkeys, Pilgrims, and pumpkins. The cornucopia (*korn-yoo-KOH-pee-uh*), or "horn of plenty," is a symbol for the Thanksgiving harvest. This cone-shaped horn is often filled with fruits, nuts, vegetables, and sometimes even flowers. Did you know that the original cornucopia was made of a hollow goat's horn? It's true!

Knock, knock.

Who's there?

Hornet.

Hornet who?

Hornet plenty.

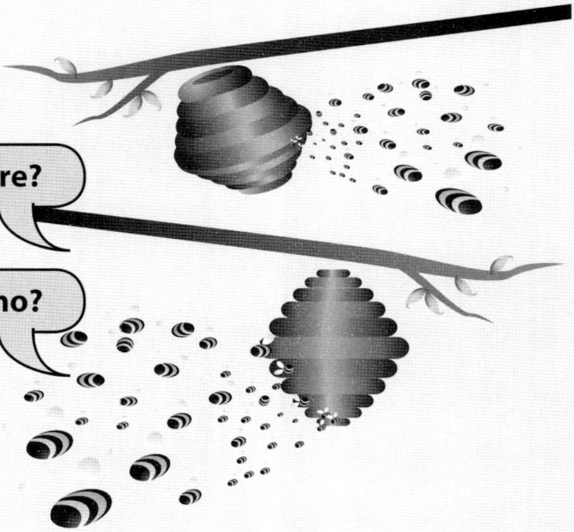

Knock, knock.

Who's there?

Avery.

Avery who?

Avery body needs to help set the table.

All afternoon eight angry ants ate eight awful apples.

Limerick

There was a girl named Eleanor.
Indian corn she hung on her door.
Some crows came along,
Croaking their song—
Now the corn on her door is no more!

FUN FACT

Indian corn is a Thanksgiving symbol. Several ears of colorful Indian corn tied together with a ribbon may be hung as a decoration during the Thanksgiving season. Indian corn reminds people of how the Wampanoag Indians taught the Pilgrims how to grow corn. Did you know that these Native Americans grew corn for more than just food? It's true! They wove the husks into mats.

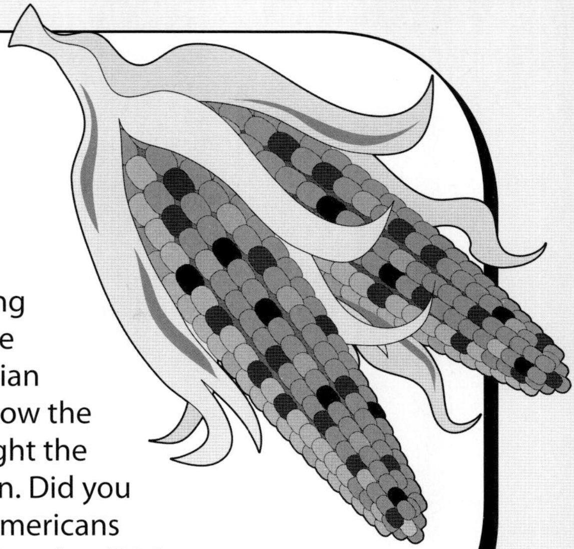

Knock, knock.

Who's there?

Albee.

Albee who?

Albee there for dinner.

What are unhappy cranberries called?

Blueberries.

8 Autumn

Why do so many people shop for cars around Thanksgiving?

It's a good time to buy an autumn-mobile.

Knock, knock.

Who's there?

Theresa.

Theresa who?

Theresa green until autumn.

Why is Thanksgiving such a smart holiday?

Because it's in Know-vember.

Which month has 28 days?

All of them.

DID YOU KNOW?

In autumn in some parts of the world, the leaves turn red, yellow, and orange. But did you know that these are the leaves' natural colors? That's right! As the days become shorter, the plants have less time to make food, and the green begins to disappear. The leaves' real colors are revealed. The trees get ready to rest for the winter months ahead.

What did one autumn leaf say to the other?

"I'm falling for you."

Limerick

There once was a tree whose bright hues
Were displayed in three colors so true.
Oh, what a sight!
We thought the tree might
Turn completely to red, white, and blue.

Knock, knock.

Who's there?

Woo.

Woo who?

Woo who! We have the day off from school!

Lots of large leaves littered Lara's little lawn.

Knock, knock.

Who's there?

Scold.

Scold who?

Scold outside.

Rita's nice neighbor never remembers "November before December."

Limerick

There are just a few things to remember
About the autumn month of November.
The leaves will all fall
And it's not at all
Like the short chilly days in December.

9 Football

Why did the turkey run out onto the football field?

Because the ref called a fowl.

Why did the football join the game?

He got a kick out of it.

How do football players stay cool during the game?

They stand near the fans.

DID YOU KNOW?

Did you know that footballs were once made from the bladders of pigs? It's true. They were called pigskins because no one wanted to say they were playing with a bladder! Later, the bladder was covered with leather. This gave the ball more strength. But the large size and shape of the early footballs did not make them easy to throw. This became a problem when the rules changed and passing was allowed for the first time in 1906.

DID YOU KNOW?

Did you know that the Thanksgiving Day football tradition started in 1934 when the Detroit Lions played the Chicago Bears in the University of Detroit Stadium? It's true. At that time, football players did not have to wear helmets! Football helmets were not required until the rules changed and players were allowed to tackle below the waist.

Phil footed five field goals.

Knock, knock.

Who's there?

Hal.

Hal who?

Hal for a touchdown!

Why was Cinderella such a poor football player?

She had a pumpkin for a coach.

Knock, knock.

Who's there?

Cheryl.

Cheryl who?

Cheryl leaders
cheer loud!

Why was Cinderella thrown off the football team?

Because she ran from the ball.

Limerick

There was a young player named Cole.
The other team's football he stole.
They went for a sack
And got the ball back,
Then they kicked the winning field goal.

What's the best way to catch a football?

Have somebody throw it to you.

Tall Tim threw three terrific touchdowns.

FUN FACT

The first football helmets were made of padded leather and had no facemasks. They were available to college players in 1933, although many players chose not to wear them. It wasn't until 1939 that college players had to wear helmets. Just a few years later, professional football players were required to wear them as well. In 1948 the first logo, the Rams horns, were painted on a pro leather helmet.

Limerick

While playing a game of football,
The ref made a really bad call.
The players all quit,
And said, "This is it.
We're not coming back till next fall!"

Why did the football coach go to the bank?

To get his quarterback.

Knock, knock.

Who's there?

Pig.

Pig who?

Pig me to be on your football team!

10 Thanksgiving Day Parade

What type of music do balloons hate?

Pop.

What did the dentist give to the marching band?

A tuba toothpaste.

What instrument goes *ring-ring*?

A saxo-phone.

Both big blue balloons blew by Broadway buildings.

DID YOU KNOW?

Each year, the Macy's Thanksgiving Day Parade marches through New York City. But did you know this parade actually started out as a Christmas parade? That's' right. The Macy's Christmas Parade was held on November 27, 1924. Santa Claus, who appeared at the end of the parade, was a sign that the holiday season had begun. The name was later changed to the Macy's Thanksgiving Day Parade—but Santa still appears at the end.

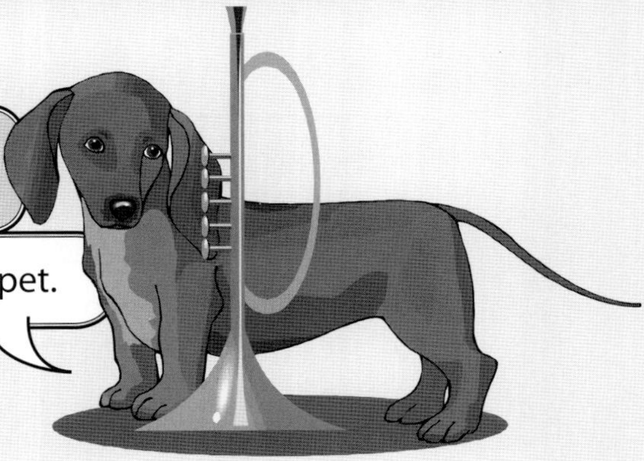

What is the loudest pet?

The trum-pet.

Knock, knock.

Who's there?

Rosa.

Rosa who?

Rosa drummers marched.

How do you make a bandstand?

Take away the chairs.

What is the most musical bone?

The trom-bone.

FUN FACT

Five giant character balloons were used in the 1928 Macy's Christmas Parade. Did you know that at the end of the parade the balloons were given slow leaks? They were then let go into the sky. It would take about one week for the balloons to fall back to the ground. Attached to the balloons were waterproof envelopes with reward information inside. It's true! Macy's offered a reward of $100 for each balloon returned safely. In 1929, ten balloons were released, with a $50 reward for each balloon's return.

Limerick

There was an old man named Pete
Who always marched down our street.
Knees high in the air,
Wind blowing his hair,
And never with shoes on his feet.

Four fancy floats finished first Friday.

Knock, knock.

Who's there?

Norma Lee.

Norma Lee who?

Norma Lee I watch the Thanksgiving Day Parade on TV.

Limerick

There was a boy so tall and proud,
He always stood out in a crowd.
He played in the band,
Which gave him a hand
For playing his horn twice as loud.

Fun Activity

How to Write a Fun Limerick

A limerick is a funny, rhyming poem that is five lines long. Lines 1, 2, and 5 rhyme. Lines 3 and 4 are usually shorter and rhyme with each other.

It's easy to write a limerick of your own. First, brainstorm some rhyming words. Write them down on a piece of paper. Example: France, dance, pants, ants, true, knew, too, blue. Next, number lines on a piece of paper from 1 to 5. Write lines 1 and 2 so that the last word in line 2 rhymes with the last word in line 1.

Example:

1. There once was a man from France.
2. His friends thought he liked to dance.

Then write lines 3 and 4 so that the last word in line 4 rhymes with the last word in line 3.

Example:

3. But that was not true
4. And what no one knew

Finally, write line 5 so the last word rhymes with lines 1 and 2.

Example:

5. Was he really had ants in his pants.

Limericks are fun to write on your own or with a group of people.

Words to Know

feast—A very large meal, usually attended by a lot of people.

harvest—To gather a crop such as pumpkins or corn.

joke—Something that is said to make people laugh.

limerick—A funny poem that is five lines long, where lines 1, 2, and 5 rhyme and are seven to ten syllables; and lines 3 and 4 rhyme and are four to six syllables.

Mayflower—The small wooden ship in which the Pilgrims sailed.

pardon—For Thanksgiving, to allow a doomed turkey to live instead of being served for dinner.

Pilgrims—People who traveled to a new place looking for a better life.

settlers—People who move to a new place, like the Pilgrims did in 1620.

tongue twister—Fun words that when put together can be hard to say.

tradition—A belief or custom handed down over the years.

Read More

Books

Dahl, Michael, Kathi Wagner, Aubrey Wagner, and Aileen Weintraub. *The Everything Kids' Giant Book of Jokes, Riddles & Brain Teasers.* Avon, MA: F + W Media, 2010.

Leno, Jay. *How to Be the Funniest Kid in the Whole World (or Just in Your Class).* New York: Aladdin Paperbacks, Simon & Schuster Children's Publishing, 2007.

Phillips, Bob. *Super Incredible Knock-Knock Jokes for Kids.* Eugene, OR: Harvest House Publishers, 2007.

Internet Addresses

DreamBox Learning: Pumpkin Math Jokes
<http://www.dreambox.com/blog/pumpkin-math-jokes>

National Geographic Kids: First Thanksgiving
<http://kids.nationalgeographic.com/kids/stories/history/first-thanksgiving/>

Index